C000015679

THE
Archive Photographs
SERIES

ALBRIGHTON
AND
SHIFNAL

The quiet country village of Albrighton before the First World War, and before the motor-car changed everything.

The Market Place in Shifnal, dominated by the railway bridge, which brought the railway through, or rather above the town, from 1849.

THE
Archive Photographs
SERIES

ALBRIGHTON
AND
SHIFNAL

Compiled by
Alec Brew

CHALFORD

First published 1996
Copyright © Alec Brew, 1996

The Chalford Publishing Company
St Mary's Mill, Chalford,
Stroud, Gloucestershire, GL6 8NX

ISBN 0 7524 0384 2

Typesetting and origination by
The Chalford Publishing Company
Printed in Great Britain by
Redwood Books, Trowbridge

St Bartholomew's church, Tong, one of the loveliest of all English village churches, and the place chosen by Charles Dickens as the 'burial site' of his fictional heroine Little Nell, in *The Old Curiosity Shop*.

Contents

Tong Castle, the third on the site, having been built by George Durant in 1765, and finally demolished in 1954 having been derelict for some time.

Park Farm, Kingswood in the 1920s, and a 'crop' of over ninety rabbits from just one wheatfield. Left to right: Alfred Hughes, Tom Ellis, and his father, also named Tom Ellis.

Introduction

Sandwiched between the industrial conurbation of Wolverhampton and the Black Country, and the even older industrial towns which now make up Telford, lies a quiet rural area in which the two main settlements are Albrighton and Shifnal. Though now having roughly the same populations, Shifnal was once rather bigger and regarded as a town, whereas Albrighton has always been seen as a village. Equally though, they served the agricultural areas around them, and it was in agriculture that most of the local population used to be engaged.

The area remained almost untouched by the growth of industry on each side, even after the Wolverhampton to Shrewsbury railway line was opened in 1849, cutting right through the region. It was not until after the First World War that a significant change began to take place. Then the growth of mechanisation in agriculture and the lure of higher paid jobs in industry, lead to a steady change in emphasis as the area became more a dormitory for its neighbours.

There was even a small decline in the population between the Wars, but then housing estates began to be built in Albrighton and Shifnal, and more people began to commute out of the area, a process which accelerated with the growth of car ownership.

One development which bucked the trend was the construction of RAF Cosford in 1938, as the home of No. 2 School of Technical Training and No. 9 Maintenance Unit, immediately between Albrighton and Shifnal. Cosford became a large employer of locallabour and still is to this day, as it became the sole RAF base for the training of ground technicians.

Around Albrighton and Shifnal are a number of smaller villages, still almost entirely agricultural in nature, and the most famous of these is Tong. There are two reasons why such a small village has had so much written about it, apart from its attractiveness, the first is the flight of King Charles after the battle of Worcester, and his seeking refuge in the farmhouse at Whiteladies Priory, and then at Boscobel House, hiding there in a priest's hole, and in the branches of an oak tree in the forest.

The second reason for Tong's fame is more fanciful, it is believed to be setting for Little Nell's home village in Charles Dickens' novel *The Old Curiosity Shop*.

Of the other villages covered in this book, perhaps the least changed by the passage of time is Beckbury. Hidden at the end of narrow lanes it still retains something of the nature of Albrighton as it used to be, though on a smaller scale. With village life centred on the church, village hall, primary school and the Seven Stars public house and without any large new housing developments, Beckbury is still the quiet close-knit rural community which Shifnal and Albrighton used to be. Only the lack of a shop has changed the nature of life in the village, and made owning a car almost a necessity.

The village of Donington is almost a suburb of Albrighton, physically linked to it, but with its own church, St Cuthbert's, only a stone throw from St Mary Magdalene in Albrighton. Donington also had its own school, to which my great-grandfather, George, trudged each day from Tong Castle, where his father was gamekeeper, but it has been a nursery school for around thirty years.

Another little school which no longer functions is at the top of the common in Kingswood, alongside the little church which is now all part of a private dwelling. Kingswood is a curious place, large in area but small in population, built along two main roads, and across the county line. The first of its two pubs, Croakers Wine Bar, or The Junction as it once was, sits in a fork of the A 41 and marks the beginning of the area on the road from Wolverhampton.

Haymaking in Newhouse Lane, Albrighton in the early 1920s. Left to right: Mr Pitchford, George Jordon, Frank Hodgkiss and Bill Carrington,

One

Albrighton

The epitome of a large English country village, Albrighton dates back to Saxon times, and by the time the Domesday Book was compiled there were already 480 acres under cultivation. Serving the local agricultural community Albrighton has grown steadily over the years, but has mushroomed in population since the Second World War as the area became a dormitory for Wolverhampton and the Black Country.

With its pleasant tree-lined High Street, returned to some of its former quietness after the building of the bypass, though spoiled somewhat by the construction of some new shops and houses in the 1950s, Albrighton has all the facilities a self-contained village needs, including a railway station.

The Crown public house, usually regarded as the centre of the village, at the cross-roads of High Street, Cross Street and Station Road.

A class at the Manor House School sometime during the last century. Dora Hill is the girl seated on the extreme left.

The High Street, around the turn of the century, looking towards the distant church. The house in the foreground later became the Bush public house, and the building in the background with the tall chimney was a millers which later became Lockley's garage.

VALUABLE FREEHOLD ESTATE,

SHROPSHIRE,

ADJOINING THE HOLYHEAD ROAD, MIDWAY BETWEEN WOLVERHAMPTON AND SHIFFNAL.

TO BE

Sold by Auction,

BY

R. S. WALKER,

On THURSDAY, the 2nd of June, 1836,

AT THE HOUSE OF MR. JONES, WHISTON CROSS INN,

IN THE COUNTY OF SALOP AFORESAID,

PRECISELY AT 4 o'CLOCK IN THE AFTERNOON, SUBJECT TO SUCH CONDITIONS AS WILL BE THEN PRODUCED.

ALL THAT TRULY VALUABLE

FREEHOLD ESTATE,

SITUATE AT BONINGALE,

AND LATE IN THE OCCUPATION OF Mr. GEORGE SUTTON, DECEASED.

CONTAINING 51A. 2R. 0P. OR THEREABOUTS, OF EXCELLENT

ARABLE, PASTURE, TURNIP, & MEADOW LAND,

IN A HIGH STATE OF CULTIVATION, TOGETHER WITH THE

FARM HOUSE, BARNS, STABLES,

COW HOUSES, MALT HOUSE, TWO COTTAGES,

AND OTHER APPURTENANCES.

Mr. BOULTON, of Humphreston Hall, will upon application shew the Estate, and for Information apply to Mr. J. B. FARMER, Solicitor, or the AUCTIONEER, both of Wolverhampton.

PRICE, PRINTER, NEW TOWN, BILSTON.

The sale of a small farm in 1836 on the death of the owner, George Sutton. The farm was sited at Boningale, but arrangements to show people round were with John Boulton from Humphreston Hall.

Albrighton National School in 1847. The only known person is the little girl marked with a cross who is one of the Hill girls, probably Minnie.

The celebration of May Day was an important village event. This is the May Day Committee about 1913. Left to right: Mr Stroudly, Mr W. Cottam, Dr A. Lamb, Mr Yates, Revd P.R. Bartley, Mr J. Wilcox, Mr H. Morris, Mr G. Jordan, -?-, -?-.

The girls of Albrighton celebrating May Day around the years 1910-12. This used to be a regular feature of village life.

The May Queen and her entourage setting off on their procession through the village. Note that that the 'retainers' holding up the canopy are blacked up.

Albrighton, Manor House.

A young lad standing in the exact centre of the village in front of the Crown, with the Manor House behind him. He would not stand there very long these days without being run down.

Playing croquet on the Manor House lawn, at some time before the First World War. The Crown is visible over the wall.

The staff of Albrighton railway station, date unknown. Built in 1848 by the Shrewsbury and Birmingham Railway, it was taken over in 1853 by the Great Western Railway. Today, of course, the station is unmanned.

Dartmouth Terrace in Shaw Lane, built in 1897, and pictured not long afterwards. Elias Nott is by the gate of the first house, and the boy in the floppy hat is Charles Henry (Harry) Nott.

A well known Albrighton family taken around the turn of the century. Standing left to right: Harry Nott (later owner of the toy and model shop), Elias Nott (builder), Lizzie Nott (teacher), George Nott (garage owner and ironmonger), and their parents William Nott (builder and undertaker) and Annie Nott.

Bert Lockley outside his garage in 1917-18, not long after opening it. He was an agent for AJS motor-cycles, and appears to sell Dunlop and Goodyear tyres and Mobil oil and petrol.

Hugh Pierpoint, Albrighton village postman in 1919.

Harry Nott's wedding picture. He is wearing his DFM, awarded for action when flying as observer in a BE.2C on 19 January 1916. When his aircraft was attacked by two German Taubes, despite being hit in the eye by shrapnel he continued firing and shot down one of the Germans and drove off the other.

Albrighton Infants School in 1922-23. The teacher on the left is Miss Bishton, and on the right is Hilda Smith, the headmaster's wife.

Albrighton Hall, which is now at the opposite end of the village to the original hall, which was in the area near the Shrewbury Arms, though exactly where is not clear, it was abandoned in the sixteenth century.

The May Queen celebrations in 1926, on the vicarage lawn. The Revd Green is at the rear, and Mrs Hilda Smith is in the hat in front of one of the windows.

The road from Tong up to the Shrewsbury Arms, and known as The Dog Bank because the pub was widely known as 'The Dog' at the time, because of the hound on the Talbot family arms hanging outside.

The Shrewsbury Arms at the north end of the High Street, by the junction of Church Street.

This delightful group of Brownies in the 1920s includes a boy, George Windsor at the back. Joan Nott (now Joan Lees) is centre right.

These are the Albrighton Girl Guides at about the same time. On the left is Miss Godfrey and on her right Miss Russell.

The eldest of three class groups from Albrighton School in the early 1920s. Left to right, back row: F. Garvey. G. Perry, G. Giles, -?-, G. Mountford, -?-, G. Davis, B. Royal. Second row: B. Richards, G. Garvey, M. Shingler, -?-, Mr Reginald Smith (headmaster), ? Roberts, D. Jones, -?-, Floss Cottam. Third row: J. Gallimore, I, Davis, K. Garvey, J. Harper, G. Davis, B. Cotterill, ? Royal, -?-. Front row: Eric Moore, Alex Brown, T. Stockton, G. Pugh, A. Preece, G. Lycett, -?-.

The middle group of children. Left to right, back row: Harold Mountford, C. Jones, J. Preece, G. Cotterell, J. Head, -?-, I. Lockley. Second row: N. Nott, -?-, M. Nicklin, -?-, -?-, Reginald Smith, E. Nicklin, M. Bodin, ? Reynolds, -?-. Third row: -?-, -?-, I. Royal, -?-, B. Ellis, S. Simpson, -?-, W. Garvey. Front row: -?-, J. Jarman, Fred Evans, -?-, ? Unit, G. Hill, ? Gallimore, Chris Mason.

The infants at the same time. Left to right, back row: Bob Smith, J. Head, ? Bodin, ? Preece, Ted Jones, Horace Lockley. Second row: M. Broome, Gwen Moore, ? Reynolds, B. Owen, -?-, Molly Jordon, -?-. Third row: Cliff Royal, Mable Nott, ? Davis, Ada Hill, Winnie Cornes, -?-. Front row: ? Simpson, Tom Hill, T. Cotterill.

The High Street before 1911, Miller's stores on the right, and the Crown is central in the distance.

St Mary Magdalene church and the verger's cottage. The oldest part of the church, the tower, was built in the twelfth century. The local clockmaker, John Baddeley installed the first clock in 1790, and there were face renewals in 1872 and 1969.

The interior of St Mary Magdalene church before the First World War. There was a major reconstruction during 1993.

Janet Grieg by the Green, in front of the Harp in 1926. The Grieg's lived on a farm down a lane to the left of the Kingswood Road. The first house on the right was Miss Dimelow's infants school.

Albrighton cricket team 1923-24. Left to right, back row: Jack Pitchford, -?-, Charlie Bucknall, Bill Pearson, (capt.), Fred Allen. Seated row: -?-, Ernest Smith, Rev Bartlett, -?-, -?-, -?-. Front row: -?-.

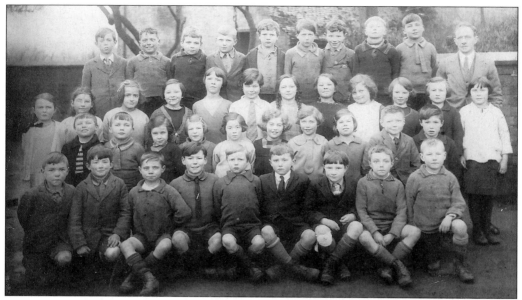

Another photograph of the children at Albrighton School, from around 1927. Left to right, back row: Harry Walker, Jim Cotterill, Stan Jones, George Windsor, Jim Preece, -?-, Bob Smith, Billy Bowden, Llewelyn Head, Reginald Smith. Second row: Sophie Moore, Bertha Lycett, Nellie Elcock, Joyce Jordon, ? Hunt, Mary Bromley, Barbara Owen, Glayds ?, Emily Preece, Gwen Davis, Gwen Moore, ? Pooler. Third row: Ralph Hunt, Bernard Head, Joan Nott, Mary Broome, Ada Hill, Mable Nott, Winnie Cornes, Ginny Davis, Eric Wooldridge, Billy Simpson. Front row: Cliff Royal, Tom Hill, Joe Cotterill, George Cornes, Horace Lockley, Humphrey Barnes, Billy Garvey, Ted Jones, ? Pooler.

The May Queen procession through the town. The May Queen is riding on milkman, Alf Gibson's horse. The 'Knight in Shining Armour', George Windor, is on his grandfather's pony, his grandfather being the ex-stationmaster.

The High Street looking from the Green by the Harp towards the centre of the village, probably some time late in the last century.

A view looking at the same corner of the High Street from the other end.

Another view of the High Street. The two children on the right are in the doorway of Forshaw's the clothiers, and the shops on the left have now been replaced by the Miller's Green flats.

Albrighton church from the other side of Albrighton Pool, or Donington Pool, depending on which side you live. Albrighton Brook, which was dammed to form the pool, is the parish boundary, so the pool lies in both parishes.

The 1927 May Day procession about to set off. The first five children are Sophie Moore, Joan Nott, Megan Gallimore, Cliff Royal and Gwen Moore. Mrs Bishton with her back to the camera and Reginald (Dickie) Smith are supervising the May Queen's entourage.

Two little girls on May Day, awaiting the Maypole dancing, Emily Priest on the left and one of the Pooler girls, with Joan Nott looking on from the right.

Another school group, around 1932. Left to right, back row: Joe Cotterill, Jack Davies, George Cornes, Stan Jones, Horace Lockley, -?-, Bernard Head, Humphrey Barnes, -?-, Billy Simpson, John Brew. Second row: -?-, Vera ?, a Hogarth twin, -?-, a Heighway twin, Emily Preece, Reginald Smith, Marjorie Morris, a Heighway twin, Kathleen Reynolds, Gwen Moore. Third row: Violet Lockley, Dot Morris, a Hogarth twin, Molly Jordan, -?-, Joan Titley, Sophie Moore. Front row: Bob Barnes, Joyce Dimelow, Betty Taffenden, Marie Reskin, Mary Lewis, Doreen Bourne, Mable Leadbetter, -?-.

Another May Day procession through the village, though in this one the May Queen's steed is not being lead by an adult, and her Knight in Shining Armour is having a walk.

Mable Nott and Bob Smith (the headmaster's son) about to start off on the May Day procession.

The Revd Green crowning Maud Titley (now Maud Hawksworth, secretary of the Albrighton Historical Society) as the May Queen.

A Women's Institute performance in 1927. Standing left to right: Miss Cole, Miss Allen, Miss Alice Mason, Miss Pearson, Miss Russell, and seated, Miss Renney, Miss Doris Pierpoint, Miss Jordan and Miss Bassett.

The Albrighton Band in 1935 outside the Harp public house. Their uniforms came secondhand from the Lilleshall Colliery Band, and the bandmaster, fourth from the left was Charles Howells.

The Albrighton Women's Institute parading on the occasion of the Silver Jubilee in 1935.

G.A. & C.H. Nott's ironmongers
decorated for George VI's Coronation.
This is now the Spar shop.

A Morris Commercial Leader belonging to Millward Bros, who operated the Malthouse in Station Road, opposite the school. This burnt down in 1959.

The workshop at Albrighton School in 1935. Dickie Smith encouraged village children to learn to use their hands and items built by the boys regularly won prizes at a Shrewsbury Show. This happened so often that other schools protested and the competitions were stopped and replaced by exhibitions.

The girls of Albrighton School show off their gymnastic prowess in 1936.

A cooking class from the school in the Wesley Hall, before the Second World War. During the war the Wesley Hall was regularly used by the increased numbers of children in the village brought about by an influx of evacuees.

Scrivens shop in the Old Post Office, in the High Street, probably before the First World War.

Nott's cycle shop decorated for George V's Silver Jubilee in 1935.

'Phone 10 Albrighton.

Established over 50 Years.

F. R. SCRIVEN,

Grocer, Baker, Corn and Meal Factor,
Wine and Spirit Merchant,

ALBRIGHTON.

The Noted Shop for
HOME-CURED Cottage Fed
BACON and HAMS,
matured to perfection.

Our PORK PIES
are noted throughout the Midlands.

Tea Parties catered for with Fields for playing and
large Hall for wet weather.   Also Parties provided
with Field and Hot Water.

We carry an extensive Stock of

PATENT MEDICINES,

Children's Food,

CATTLE MEDICINES,

Cooper's Sheep Dips & Specialities,
Sherleys' & Bob Martin's
Dog Powders, etc.

For ALL CLASSES of BUILDING WORK
REPAIRS, RENOVATIONS, etc.

Consult

PHONE 24 **W. NOTT** ESTAB^D 1881.
ALBRIGHTON.

PLUMBING, PAINTING & DECORATING.
ESTIMATES FREE.   FUNERALS FURNISHED.

THE "HARP" HOTEL,
ALBRIGHTON.

This popular house has now a new tenant —
MOSES SCOTT,
who, for many years, has been "mine host" at
THE ROSE & CROWN, PENN.

"Mo" and Mrs. Scott will give a warm
welcome to old friends and new.

TELEPHONE : ALBRIGHTON 123.

ANNE BAILEY,

HIGH-CLASS LADIES' AND
CHILDREN'S HAIRDRESSER

Permanent Waving Specialist

31, HIGH STREET, ALBRIGHTON.

A number of Albrighton businesses advertising in the Silver Jubilee brochure in 1935.

The 10th Salop Battalion of the Home Guard's Stand Down party in the Assembly Rooms, Albrighton 14 December 1944. Sergeant Harry Nott is the first one from the left, in glasses.

A British Legion Empire Day dance, date unknown. Front row, left to right: Mrs Scriven, Harold Srciven, -?-, John Rennie, Mrs George Nott, Reg Windsor, Mrs Windsor, -?-, Dolly Bassett.

The Sunday school teachers and ladies of the parish church council in February 1943. Back row, left to right: Mrs Stirk, Mrs Brown, Mrs Bromley, Miss Boddison, Revd W. Devenish, Mrs Miller, Mrs Heately. Font row: Mrs Perrins, Mrs Thompson, Mrs Hawksworth, Miss Lamb, Miss Morris, Mrs Meddings.

Class 2 at what had by this time become just an infants school in Station Road, 1954-55. The New Albrighton County Junior School had opened in 1952 on the other side of the village.

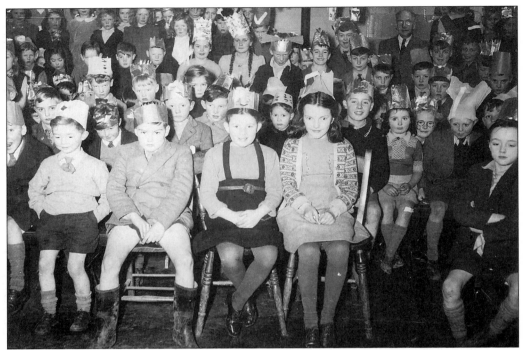

A post-war children's party in the Assembly Rooms. Most of them look pretty miserable, especially the boy in the wellies!

Albrighton Post Office staff in the 1940s. Back row, left to right: Mr Andrews, Mrs Bates, Mrs Gunnell, Mrs Caddick, Mr Garvey, Mr Pell. Front row: Mrs Amos, Mrs Williams (postmistress), Mrs Howells.

Miss Ethel Nicklin cycling from the Crown on a cold winter's day in the late 1950s.

The Albrighton WVS, best team in Salop in 1959, and second in the British Isles. Back row: Nancy Bushell, Molly Cook, Gwen Matthews, -?-. Front row: Mrs Aston, Mrs Jones, -?-, Dora Allen, Mrs Joan Lenthall.

An early aerial view of Albrighton County School, fully completed in 1953, it had become necessary to occupy part of it in 1951 because of the mushrooming village population. Note the nearness of RAF Cosford, and the roof of St Cuthbert's Grange in the grove of trees in the background, now the housing estate, Grange Park.

The teaching and meal staff at the new school in 1952. Back row, left to right: -?-, -?-, -?-, Mr Edwards, -?-, -?-, Mrs Kinnings, -?-. Front row: Miss Kendrick, Mr Dyer, Mr A.R. Matthias (headmaster), Mrs Clarke, Mr Firfield.

The first PTA Board of Managers of Albrighton County School in 1952.

Mrs Clark's first and second year transition class, June 1953. The sculpture on the left was by Dr Vogel.

An exiting finish during sports day in 1954.

Mrs Legge, Chairman of Managers (the wife of Dr Legge) presenting the Manager's Cup to the captains of Rodney House, Diane Yates and Christopher Powell, during the Sports Day at Cosford in July 1952. Mr Matthias is on the left and Mrs Clarke on the right.

Mr Legge, the village doctor, judging the school fancy dress competition in the summer of 1953.

Albrighton School football team in 1961-62.

Albrighton School Sports Day in 1962. A tense moment at the finish of the event.

A common finish for a sack race, as all co-ordination goes amid desperation to reach the tape.

Albrighton Junior School, Albrighton Church Sunday School party, 9 January 1965.

These Horsa assault gliders fuselages were still in use in 1968 as sheds in the timber yard at the entrance to Albrighton station. They had been sold off after the war and many became instant sheds.

The Melville Club meeting for tea and reminiscences. Formed as a Darby and Joan club in 1958 it was renamed in honour of Dr Melville Legge. Left to right: Ben Jones, Dolly Sergeant, Mr Broxton, Eric Whittingham, Gwen Matthias, Dora Allen and Flossie Stockton.

Fittingly the last picture in the Albrighton section, Armistice Day, 1971. At the War Memorial on the Dog Bank, Catherine Howells, aged seven, was the youngest person in the country to play the *Last Post*.

Two

Beckbury

Lying hidden at the end of narrow country lanes, where making way for a tractor or herd of cows is a daily hazard, Beckbury is close to being the sort of sleepy rural community that its larger neighbours used to be. With its tiny church, public house, school and village hall, it is a close-knit community in which agriculture is still the prime interest.

Though people commute to work from Beckbury, the village is still affected by the season, nature, and the taming of it, is still a part of village life; and because it offers the Seven Stars pub, Beckbury even draws people from its tiny neighbours, Badger and Ryton.

The Pennerly family wedding party in Beckbury at the turn of the century.

The Revd J.J. Daniels, rector of Beckbury from 1882 to 1910, with his son.

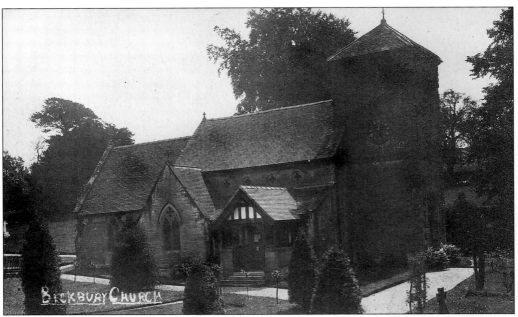

St Milburga church, Beckbury between the wars. The chancel survives from the second part of the thirteenth century, with a Georgian nave and west tower. Revd Daniels spent most of his tenure restoring the church.

The centre of Beckbury showing the old post office, with Mr Butcher in the doorway. Mr Crowther and his son Charles are standing in the road.

The Rectory at the nearby village of Badger, sometime during the last century. The family is believed to be the Leigh Lyes. The lady who is 'being mother' was obviously influenced by royal fashions at the time.

The cottages opposite the church, now occupied by the Downward and Salter families.

The front of Beckbury Hall in the 1950s with Piers Browne and Nicky Browne, and their nanny, Miss Brown, who was no relation.

Mrs Nora Thompson, Beckbury village postwoman, at the top of Beckbury Bank, around 1948.

Frances Thompson (now Mrs Frances Plain) outside the Thompson house on the left side of Beckbury Bank in 1948.

Beckbury Infant School children in 1949. On the right is Miss Higginson, the infant teacher, and Frances Thompson is in the middle row, fifth from the left.

St Andrews church, in the neighbouring village of Ryton. Set on the edge of the valley of the River Worfe, at the end of a cul-de-sac, it is a delightfully quiet location.

The Revd Bray and the Misses Sykes, Mary and Esther, outside Beckbury Hall during a village Fête in the 1950s.

The 1953 Beckbury School production. The two teachers visible are Mrs Wild on the left and Miss Higginson on the right.

Beckbury choir in 1960. Back row, left to right: David Treen, Revd Bray, Mr Davidson. Second row: Roger Treen, Peter Owen, Paul Owen, Wyndham Davidson. Third row: John Northwood, John Ford, David Smith, Chris Unit, David Turner. Front row: Terry Rhodes, Raymond Bibby, Robert Bibby, Norman Downward.

Miss Higginson and her infant class at Beckbury school in 1958.

Mrs Wild and her junior class, also in 1958.

Cottages Nos. 42 and 43 in Beckbury, and behind them the blacksmith's shop which has now gone.

A special tree planting ceremony to celebrate 100 years of Beckbury school. The little girl with the big shovel is Janet Plain, and Mr Aston, the headmaster is holding the tree.

Three

Cosford

Construction of the RAF station at Cosford began in 1938 as part of the RAF's expansion programme, and was the most dramatic change to take place in the area of Albrighton and Shifnal since the coming of the railway. Built as the home of No. 2 School of Technical Training and No.9 Maintenance Unit, the base has grown steadily over the years, and has an assured future becoming the RAF's only training station for ground-based trades.

The name of Cosford, though, is more widely known as the home of British Indoor Athletics, and is also currently the home of the Aerospace Museum, though an adjunct of the RAF Museum at Hendon, is still one of the largest and best aircraft museums in the world. Once a year Cosford's Air Display doubles the population of the region, and fills the air with noisier shapes than the Chipmunks, Bulldogs and gliders that are Cosford's more normal fare.

It is important to remember however, that Cosford village existed before the Royal Air Force took an interest in the area.

The lodge at the entrance of Cosford Grange, which can be seen in the background, before the First World War. The lodge has since been extended and the verandah around the Grange has been removed.

SYDNAL.

NEAR ALBRIGHTON, SALOP.

SALE

OF VALUABLE

FARMING STOCK,

AND

IMPLEMENTS IN HUSBANDRY,

THE PROPERTY OF J. JONES, Esq.

ON THURSDAY, MARCH 9th, 1854.

WILLIAM JONES,

AUCTIONEER.

IMPLEMENTS.

LOT		£.	s.	d
1	Sundry small tools and implements			
2	Pair of one horse harrows			
3	Pair of two ditto			
4	Pair of three ditto			
5	Turnip scuffle			
6	Ditto			
7	Ditto			
8	Ox harrow			
9	Four corn coffers, in lots			
10	Wheel barrow			
11	Pair of twins			
12	Four-horse scuffle			
13	Single iron plough			
14	Ditto			
15	Ditto			
16	Ditto			
17	Wood double plough			
18	Iron ditto			
19	Ridge plough			
20	Ditto			
21	Bentall's grubber or subsoil plough....			
22	Two wood cow cribs			
23	Two iron ditto			
24	Two horse roll			
25	Three ditto			
26	Scutch rake			
27	Two turnip slicers for cows			
28	Reaping machine			
29	Croskill's clod crusher			
30	Winnowing machine			
31	Capital straw engine			
32	Ditto			
33	Clover seed drill			
34	Double ridge turnip ditto with shafts			
35	Avery's patent weighing machine			
36	Capital six inch wheel tumbrel			
37	Four & half-inch Scotch cart			
38	Ditto			
39	Ditto			
40	Capital broad wheel waggon, double and single shafts and thripples complete			
41	Three inch ditto			
42	Ditto			

Part of a sale catalogue dating from 1854. Sydnal Farm was located on the site currently occupied by RAF Cosford's outside sports stadium.

Ernest Smith inside Cosford signal box in 1955-56.

In 1938 strange new shapes began appearing in the landscape between Albrighton and Shifnal as Sir Alfred McAlpine & Sons Ltd began building RAF Cosford as the home of No. 2 School of Technical Training.

Many of the curved Lamella concrete hangars (casting no shadows) were built around the new base, and covered with turf. They were to be used for aircraft storage by No. 9 Maintenance Unit, the other main resident of RAF Cosford.

Also constructed were these D Type hangers in a curved row on the north side of the airfield. Note the steam-powered crane mounted on rails.

Some of RAF Cosford's houses under construction in December 1938. These spread on both sides of the Albrighton to Tong road.

Two of the Lamella hangers under construction in August 1939, with war just a month away. This shows how the concrete was poured on in sections.

A steamroller in front of an almost complete Lamella, with just the end wall to finish, and the covering of turf to apply. Before the war boys from Albrighton, including my father, used to wander across the whole of this area, bird-nesting.

The main part of RAF Cosford on the other side of the railways from the airfield, includes a host of wooden huts, many of which are still in use, and the four large workshop buildings in the background, one of which became the Indoor Athletics Arena in the 1960s.

Among the huge numbers of recruits which passed through RAF Cosford during the war were a number of Football League players, giving Cosford a pretty good football team. These are the Birmingham League Champions for 1940-41. Back row, left to right: Sgt. O'Donell (Aston Villa), Sgt. Smith (Chelsea), Sgt. Bert Williams (Walsall and later Wolves), AC Young (Huddersfield), Capt. Acquana (Hull). Front row: Cpl. Sims (Wellington), AC Farell (Brighton), Staaley, Sgt. Hill (Blackpool), Cpl. Hill (Dulwich Hamlet), Sgt. Newman (Walsall).

A Boulton Paul Type D twin 0.5 in. machine gun tail turret, with radar, attached to a Halifax for trials at Cosford in February 1944. In the background are a number of Wellington bombers.

A Spitfire Mk. 22, PK722, one of the largest number broken up for scrap at Cosford in 1955-56. This one was Castle Bromwich-built. Local boys no longer went birdnesting at Cosford, but they did go aircraft spotting.

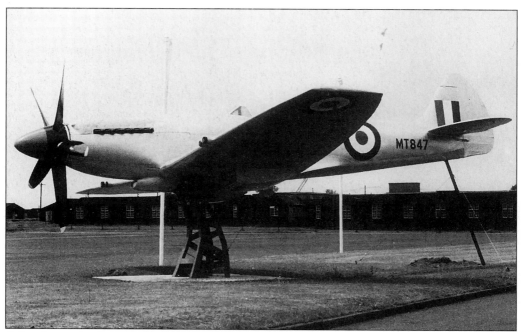

A Spitfire with a happier fate. This Mk. XIV, MT847, was a parade ground ornament for many years, but was then retired to the Aerospace Museum.

The most familiar flying scene at Cosford during the post-war years. A Slingsby T.31B Cadet glider, WT903, of the Air Training Corps being readied for launch.

A view of Cosford from a glider c. 1960, obviously in bumpy air judging by the camera shake. Cosford Grange is the white house on the left, and Cosford Waterworks is on the right. Albrighton Brook can be seen in the wooded valley between them. The road by-passing the waterworks had not yet been built.

The day each year when the population of the area doubles, the Cosford's annual air display. Cosford's 'Fort-type' control tower is quite unusual.

Since the War Cosford has housed a collection of historic aircraft. There, in 1965, spectators are crowding round the Kawaski Ki. 100-1b. the only example of this Japanese fighter left in the world, and now part of the Aerospace Museum collection.

For the Air Display the instructional airframes from the School of Technical Training are wheeled out into the sunshine. This is a Valetta T. Mk.3 pictured in 1968.

This is another instructional airframe, Hawker Hunter, 8002M, with shark's mouth nose art.

A Canberra B.2 outside a C Type hangar during the 1965 air display.

The Red Arrows are usually a feature of the Cosford Air Display, and the cameraman has clicked the shutter at the right moment as these two Hawks pass *very* close.

For many years Cosford was best known as the home of British indoor athletics. This is the early wooden track, and Ralph Banthorpe winning the 1967 AAA junior 220 yards indoor championship.

Cosford Indoor Arena in 1985 with many improvements, and Serge Bubka the World Record holder for the pole-vault about to clear the bar.

Part of the huge Aerospace Museum Collection at Cosford. Left to right: Andover BAC. 111 and Lockheed Neptune. Cosford is one of the largest and best aircraft museums in the world.

VC. 10 power controls and a model of the VC. 10 being presented to the Aerospace Museum by Boulton Paul employees in front of the Museum's Boulton Paul Sea Balliol. Left to right: Jack Chambers, -?-, Eddie Albrecht, Derek Eastwood (Museum Curator), F. Hewitt, Roy Cutler, D. Roberts, -?-, Les Tongue.

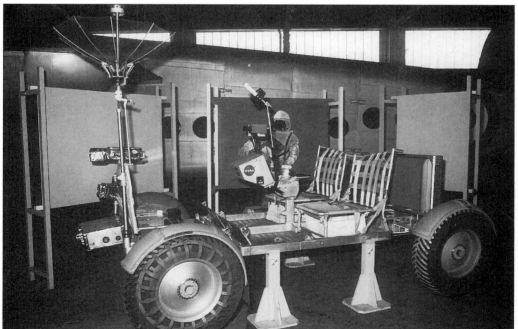

An example of NASA's moon buggy was a feature of the Aerospace Museum for many years, shown here in front of the Avro York.

Some of the more recent instructional airframes from the School of Technical Training, which has now inherited the Number One, with the closure of Halton. Seen here are Jaguars and a Buccaneer.

Some of the gliders based at Cosford in 1980, and one of the Chipmunks used as glider tugs. They are outside one of the T.2 hangers sited near the railway station.

Four
Donington

The little village of Donington lies almost as an appendage to Albrighton, becoming almost a suburb to its bigger cousin. Though its own little school closed many years ago, becoming a nursery, St Cuthbert's church remains a vibrant entity, despite being only a stone's throw away from St Mary Magdalene, Albrighton.

Often misspelled Donnington, and confused with the Telford town of the same name, Donington has struggled to retain its identity against the better known Albrighton, and it's in the fields and barns of the local farms where it's real strength lies.

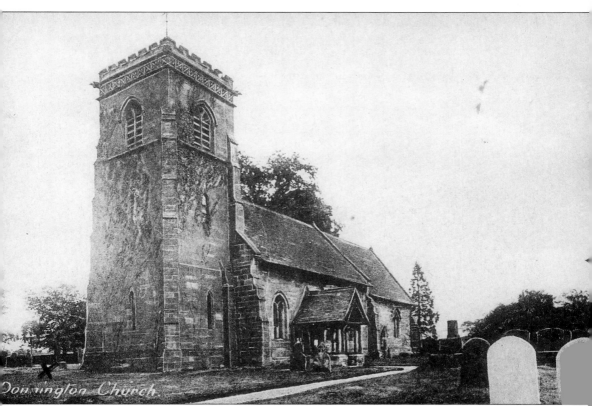

St Cuthbert's church, Donington. Even the postcard printer has made the common mistake of spelling the village 'Donnington', like the other Shropshire village of that name.

The Boulton family outside their Donington Park Farm in August 1903. Left to right standing: Connie, Charlie, Higgins; seated: Mr and Mrs John Boulton, and on the ground, H.W. Boulton.

Donington Park Farm with Mrs Boulton and her three sons outside, and two servants in the doorway. The farm is little changed today, apart from a growth of ivy.

The road from Albrighton to Donington and Tong at the turn of the century. The lodge at the entrance to St Cuthbert's Grange still stands at the end of Bowling Green Lane.

St Cuthbert's Grange, which was built in 1858-60 and was largely demolished to make way for the Grange Park housing development, though the servant's quarters, seen on the extreme right still remain.

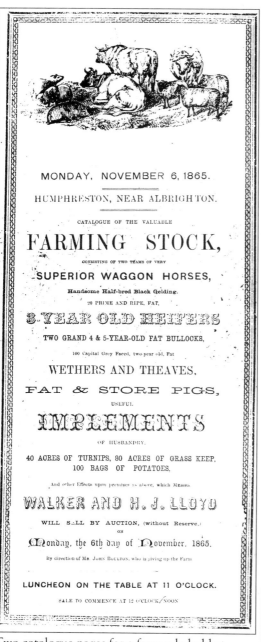

MONDAY, NOVEMBER 6, 1865.

HUMPHRESTON, NEAR ALBRIGHTON.

CATALOGUE OF THE VALUABLE

FARMING STOCK,

CONSISTING OF TWO TEAMS OF VERY

SUPERIOR WAGGON HORSES,

Handsome Half-bred Black Gelding.

20 PRIME AND RIPE, FAT,

3-YEAR OLD HEIFERS

TWO GRAND 4 & 5-YEAR-OLD FAT BULLOCKS,

100 Capital Grey Faced, two-year old, Fat

WETHERS AND THEAVES,

FAT & STORE PIGS,

USEFUL

IMPLEMENTS

OF HUSBANDRY.

40 ACRES OF TURNIPS, 80 ACRES OF GRASS KEEP, 100 BAGS OF POTATOES.

And other Effects upon premises as above, which Messrs.

WALKER AND H. J. LLOYD

WILL SELL BY AUCTION, (without Reserve,)

ON

Monday, the 6th day of November, 1865.

By direction of Mr. JOHN BOULTON, who is giving up the Farm

LUNCHEON ON THE TABLE AT 11 O'CLOCK.

SALE TO COMMENCE AT 12 O'CLOCK NOON

FAT COWS AND BULLOCKS,
(Continued.)

94	PRIME & RIPE Three-Year-Old FAT HEIFER. No.				8
95	Ditto	ditto	...	...	9
96	Ditto	ditto	...	...	10
97	Ditto	ditto	...	...	11
98	Ditto	ditto	...	...	12
99	Ditto	ditto	...	...	13
100	Ditto	ditto	...	...	14
101	Ditto	ditto	...	...	15
102	Ditto	ditto	...	...	16
103	Ditto	ditto	...	...	17
104	Ditto	ditto	...	...	18
105	Ditto	ditto	...	...	19
106	Ditto	ditto	...	...	20
107	GRAND FOUR-YEAR-OLD FAT BULLOCK				21
108	DITTO FIVE-YEAR-OLD DITTO				22

The last two lots will be sold with keep until Christmas if required.

FAT AND STORE PIGS.

109	2 FAT PIGS	...	...	...	No.	1
110	2 Ditto	...	...	...		2
111	2 Ditto	...	...	...		3
112	2 Ditto	...	...	...		4
113	2 Ditto	...	...	...		5
114	2 Ditto	...	...	...		6
115	2 Strong store ditto	...	...	...		7
116	2 Ditto ditto	...	...	...		8
117	2 Ditto ditto	...	...	...		9
118	2 Ditto ditto	...	...	...		10
119	2 Ditto ditto	...	...	...		11

GROWING TURNIPS, GRASS KEEP, POTATOES, &c.

120 FORTY ACRES OF TURNIPS, growing upon the Little Hill and Upper Coppice, to be consumed on the premises ...

121 EIGHTY ACRES OF GRASS KEEP to Lady-day next, with use of straw and foldyards ...

(In Lots to be mentioned on day of Sale.)

122 RICK of RYE GRASS ...

123 100 BAGS of WHITE ROCK POTATOES (in lots) at per bag. ...

The Auctioneers have much pleasure in calling the attention of their friends and the trade to the above important sale. The stock being of the finest quality. The Horses are especially worthy of notice, as being mostly YOUNG, SOUND, POWERFUL, and in the most USEFUL and HEALTHY CONDITION, and may be seen any time on the morning of the sale.

Two catalogue pages for a farm sale held at Humpreston Hall, near Donington in 1865. John Boulton was giving up the farm, and moving down the lane to Donington Park Farm.

The funeral of apprentice Francis Eddy from RAF Cosford in 1939 on the way to Donington church.

Arthur Parry supervising the bowls at a Donington church fête in the late 1950s.

John (J.P.) Nicholls, the blacksmith of Shackerley Lane in the late 1950s. The little boy is David Weston.

A pageant put on by members of Donington church to celebrate its 900th anniversary, in 1985. King Charles is wearing the sash, but the two Roundheads do not seem to have spotted him.

Five
Kingswood

A curious place, large in area, small in population, Kingswood lies astride a fork in the road, one road leading to Albrighton, one to Shifnal. A place then to pass through, and yet a place to visit, Kingswood Common having always drawn visitors from the town, for bare-knuckle fights in the past century, but for picnics today.

Kingswood is also astride the country boundary, most lying in Staffordshire, the rest in Shropshire. Though it had its own tiny school, older children used to go to Codsall or Albrighton schools, depending on which side of County Lane they lived.

The Junction Inn, Kingswood, now Croakers wine bar. The lady in the doorway is Mrs Lillie, and the licensee was then Mr J. Griffiths. Subsequently the pub sold Butlers Ales, and the licensee was Mr Butler (no family connection).

The Albrighton Road/County Lane crossroads before the by-pass was built. The house on the left still stands by Kingswood Common, but all the others were demolished. Left to right: the Smith's farmhouse, the Davies cottage, William Bytheway's house (he was an orphan abandoned by the roadside, hence his surname), and, just visible, Dan Brew's cottage.

Kingswood Common as it used to be, almost devoid of trees. The house on the left is now Rose Cottage, and the next is the Hodgkiss' Cottage.

Evelyn Nicklin (now Paddon) outside the Davies cottage (the Toll House) on the Staffordshire corner of County Lane. The sign says 'Pots of Tea', and the establishment catered for many visitors to Kingswood Common.

A celebrating party of ladies on Kingswood Common, occasion unknown. Back row, left to right: Miss French, Mrs Jones, Mrs Mildred Hodgkiss, Mrs Edwards, -?-, -?-. Seated: -?-, Mrs Winter (ironically the Winters kept the Summerhouse pub), -?-, -?-, -?-. On the ground Mrs Shaw and an unknown girl.

Bill Smith and his dog Scott in front of his County Lane Farm which was knocked down to make way for the Albrighton by-pass.

George Nicklin in a field next door to County Lane, with two shire horses, 'Prince' on the left and 'Darby'.

Tom Ellis of Park Farm, Kingswood, harvesting a field of wheat in 1922.

A wheelbarrow load of rabbits over ninety in number, which came out of that field. Left to right: Henry Meredith, Norman Stewart (a local solicitor out for the shooting), Hubert Ellis, Fred Meredith, Geoff Jones, Bill Meredith, Amy Meredith, and an unknown little boy in a cap.

The children of Kingswood school at the top of the common. Standing is Ruth Rimmer and Mrs Shaw, the teacher and organist at the church, and upside down are Louie Meredith and Evelyn Nicklin.

In front of the church house at the top of Kingswood Common are Bunty Meredith at the rear, Henry Meredith on the left and Hubert Ellis.

Dan Brew and his dog Razmur outside No. 5 County Lane, Kingswood. He bought the house in 1928 for £160, though he had to borrow £5 of that. It was supposed to have been demolished when Albrighton by-pass was built but he successfully contested the decision.

No. 5 County Lane being refurbished and enlarged in 1965. With the ivy removed it can be seen that it was originally a single storey stone cottage built on a piece of waste ground, with no real foundations, probably by squatters. A brick upper storey was added later. The author is in the doorway, and his brother Peter is on the scaffolding.

A group of Kingswood residents at Kingswood Poultry Farm. Standing left to right: Mrs June Ellis, Hubert Ellis, Percy Tomlinson, Mrs Urion, Tom Ellis, Bert Urion. Seated Maud Guy (*née* Ellis) and Noelle Davies.

A long standing Kingswood institution was Alfred McAlpine's plant depot, almost out of sight down a track off the Shifnal Road. This has now closed and the site is a small industrial estate.

Six

Shifnal

Most views of Shifnal are dominated by the railway bridge which looms above the Market Place, but the graceful, curved original bridge has long been replaced by the current less attractive one, Shifnal has always been the local market town, and the lure of its market brought customers in for the multitude of public houses and inns for which it has always been famous, but with the coming of the railways and the motor-car, followed by the construction of Telford just down the road, Shifnal changed irrevocably. Housing estates grew on all sides, and people came there to live here, though they worked elsewhere.

Perhaps the most unusual aspect of Shifnal, apart form its elevated railway, is the fact that it has two names. The older, but less used one, Idsall, still finds uses, not least in the name of its school, but whereas the newcomers might live in Shifnal, Shropshire, the older residents may well still live in Idsall, Salop.

The Market Place, Shifnal, dominated by the Great Western Railway bridge. T.C. Smith's sadlers shop is on the right. H. Thomason's grocer and ironmonger's under the bridge, Bennion, Horne & Marshall's stationers and bookbinders behind the group of boys and Mary Tudor's shop on the left. The group of buildings seen through the bridge have long since been cleared away.

A view of the Market Place looking away from the bridge, with T.C. Smith's on the left. The half-timbered building housing H. Haddon's was dismantled in 1936 and re-erected in Castlecroft, Wolverhampton.

The same view from further back beneath the railway bridge. The Eight Bells public house is on the left, next to the Star coaching inn which had a balcony on the roof from where approaching coaches could be spotted.

Park Street looking towards the Market Place in 1905. On the left is the Jerningham Arms, the big rival to The Star for the coaching business, and opposite is the Lloyd's Bank building.

The Broadway in 1905. The boys with the wheelbarrow have probably been asked to stand still by the photographer.

Church Street looking much as it does today, but without the double yellow lines. The white house at the end is supposed to be the oldest house in Idsall, pre-dating the fire of 1591.

St Andrew's church, Shifnal at around the turn of the century. The church dates largely from Norman times.

The interior of St Andrew's church showing the west window.

The church and its vicarage, on the opposite side of Church Street. This garden was laid out around 1841.

Haughton Hall, which lies on the Telford side of Shifnal and was started in 1718 but greatly added to in 1823-30.

Hatton Grange was built in 1764, and though lying in Shifnal parish, was in a different manor.

The Grove, Shifnal photographed at about the turn of the century.

The Shifnal station staff, together with the driver and fireman of a passing locomotive, recorded before the First World War.

Old houses formerly in the High Street and demolished after the 1920s. Council houses have been built on this site.

Haughton Lane before the First World War looking very rural. One side is now lined with houses.

Shifnal vicarage seen from the churchyard.

Shifnal Band in the 1920s before they acquired uniforms.

The Shifnal Quartet, wearing Shifnal Band uniforms. Back row, left to right: -?- and Les Haywood. Front row: Tommy Spencer and Charles Howells.

The Market Place in the 1920s. The motor-car is beginning to have its effect upon the town, with garages appearing on both sides of the road.

The front of Hatton Grange which has long been owned by the Sleaney family. It is sited on the lane towards Beckbury, near to Ryton.

Aston Hall, just off the Tong Road, was bought by the McClean family in 1865, about thirty years before this photograph was taken.

The most famous industrial unit in Shifnal was Edge & Sons wire rope and chain works, which moved there from Coalport in 1870. This is a picture of an Idsall school trip to the works in 1951.

Decker Hill House which was built by William Botfield the ironmaster around 1710. It but which is now the clubhouse of Shifnal Golf Club.

An Idsall school (then Shifnal Modern School) youth hostel trip to Ludlow in 1953.

A Shifnal Modern School production of *The Tinder Box* in December 1954. Major characters in order of appearance are: Peter Merchant, Jean Leatham, Ann Whiston, Jean Gillies, Ian Bowes, Peter Wain, Peter Manning, Geoffrey Plimley, Leslie Farndale, Michael Blythe, Leonard Davey, Patricia Druce, Mary Morris, Pamela Bothwell, Doreen Major.

Shifnal Manor, which dates from around 1400, has never had a resident Lord of the Manor, always being owned by a wealthy absentee landlords.

Shifnal Manor Pool, or Furnace Pool, was so-called because there was an early blast furnace alongside it from the late sixteenth or early seventeenth century. The pool, which was formed by damming Wesley Brook which passes through Shifnal, supplies the Manor Mill, drained in the 1960s.

The Market Place in the early post-war years, and the motor-car is having an even greater effect, though the buildings beyond the bridge have not yet been demolished to make way for a carpark.

Shifnal church viewed across the Innage through one of the railway arches.

Shifnal Second XI cricket team. Back row, left to right: John Hayward, Kevin Humphreys, Chris Shildon, David Peplow, Phil Jones, Tony Creswell, Mike Read. Front row: Ivor Peplow, -?-, Les Easthorpe, -?-, Sam Burdiss.

The Idsall School sports day July 1963 and the finish of a boy's sprint race.

Shifnal Town football team in the 1950s. The team were semi-finalist winners against A.T. & E. Bridgnorth in the Wellington League KO Cup.

The presentation evening for Shifnal Town F.C. after becoming runners-up in the Wellington League KO Cup.

Idsall School girls who took part in a December 1958 fashion show, wearing the dresses they designed and made themselves. The event was organised by K. Rowlson, the needlework teacher. The winner was Valerie Coombes.

A domestic science class at Idsall School in the late 1950s.

The Shifnal depot of Reginald Tildesley Ltd, on its opening day in May 1949, with a row of Fordson vans for sale and five company delivery vehicles.

A view of the showrooms on opening day looking out on Park House. The white tractor is a cutaway Ford Type E27N for demonstration purposes.

Inside Tildesley's workshop on opening day, with rows of pristine Ford E27N tractors and other agricultural equipment.

Reginald Tildesley's purpose built mobile workshop, which was regularly seen in Shifnal, shown here outside the main depot in Willenhall.

The captain of Shifnal cricket club's winning six-a-side team, Eddie Shelley, being presented with a cup by Bertram Hough.

Shifnal Wesleyan chapel, known as the Trinity Methodist church, was built in Victoria Street in 1880.

Shifnal Town football team before an away fixture against Coalbrookdale Old Boys in the 1960s.

Presentation night for Shifnal Town football team in the 1960s.

Shifnal cottage hospital opened in 1939 by Lady Bradford, was built on land at Lodge Hill Farm.

Shifnal cricket team second XI in 1975. Left to right, back row: Kevin Humphreys, Chris Evans, Michael Evans, Graham Evans, Andy Johnson, Mike Hayward. Front row: Paul Humpreys, Peter Mountford, Richard Upton, Peter Evens, Rene Shelley.

St Mary's church in the village of Sherrifhales.

Shifnal cricket club first XI in 1975. Left to right, back row: Tony Creswell, Barry Holhead, Graham Hills, -?-, Reg Corbishley, Edwin Broome. Front row: Phillip James, David Saffill, Peter Hulston, Brian Foulkes, Tom Clark.

Eight
Tong and Boscobel

'It was a very aged, ghostly place, the church had been built many hundreds of years ago, and had once had a convent or monastery attached, for arches in ruins, remains of oriel windows, and fragments of blackened walls, were yet standing... They admired everything, the old grey porch, the mullioned window, the venerable gravestones dotting the green churchyard, the ancient tower, the very weathercock, the brown thatched roof of cottage, barn and homestead, peeping among the trees, the streams that rippled by the distant water-mill...'

Thus did Charles Dickens describe Little Nell's home village in his book The Old Curiosity Shop, a village he based on Tong, which he had visited in the years 1850-56; but Tong had been visited by another Charles, years before, Charles Stuart, King of England, fleeing from the Parliamentary forces.

Tong Village.

The village of Tong before the First World War, and pretty well as it must have looked when Charles Dickens visited and, quite incidentally, when my great-great-great-grandfather, Thomas Brew lived there.

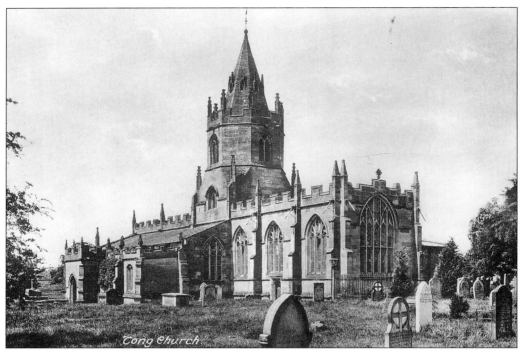

Tong church before the First World War. The present Collegiate Church was built by the widow of Sir Fulke de Pembruge, after his death in 1409. It remains one of the prettiest and most celebrated of country churches.

The interior of Tong church, photographed some time before the First World War.

The Monuments in Tong church of the Pembruge and Vernon family tombs. The nearest in view are those of Sir Fulke de Pembruge (d. 1409) and his wife Dame Elizabeth (d. 1446-7).

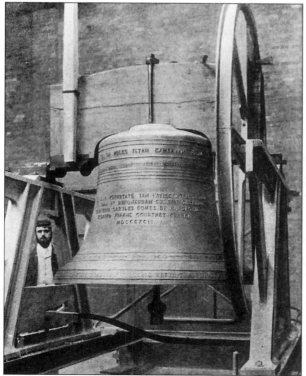

The great Bell of Tong, given to the church by Sir Henry Vernon in 1518. It was broken by Parliamentary forces in 1635, it was repaired but cracked during bell-ringing in 1848 and repaired again. Just inside the belfry are very strict instructions as to how and when the bell should be rung.

Tong vicarage, located across the road from the church, and now a very quiet road since the by-pass was built below the church.

Tong Priory, which had no religious connections at all, was a building created by George Durant of Tong Castle by constructing a new front on an existing house in 1759.

'Little Nell's Cottage'. A purely fanciful name of course, as Little Nell was a just a figment of Charles Dickens' imagination, but he is said to have based Little Nell's village on Tong, after his visit there.

The entrance to Tong Castle, which was the third to be built on the site, having been bought by George Durant from the Duke of Kingston in 1765.

Tong Castle as built by George Durant. He spent a lot on the estate and employed Capability Brown for work which included damming Neachley Brook to create Norton Mere, and Church Pool, shown here. The estate was bought by the Earl of Bradford in 1855 and as the twentieth century progressed the castle fell into ruin, not least because the lead was removed from the roof during the First World War. It became dangerous and was blown up by the army in 1954.

The domestic staff of Tong Castle at around the turn of the century. John Hartley had become the tenant of the castle and after his death in 1891 his wife continued to live there until her death in 1909.

A rear view of Tong Castle shows the mock Gothic style to good effect. When the M54 was built it went right through the site and parts of the foundation can still be seen on either side of the road, about a kilometre west of the A41.

George Durant built a number of follies around the estate in the nineteenth century and this gazebo was one, known as Tong Castle Pulpit built in 1821.

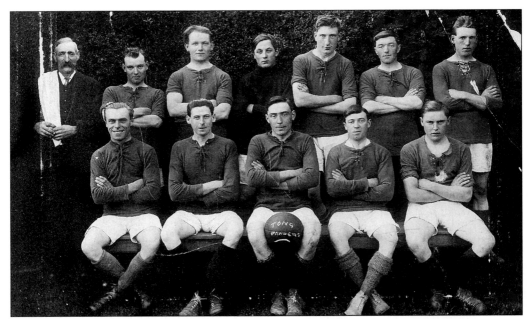

Tong Wanderers football team in the 1920s (not Tong Wanders, as spelt on the ball). Left to right, back row: Mr Wedge, J. Wynn, -?-, -?-, B. Wedge, Bert Evans, Moggy Lawrence. Front row: -?-, Harry Ball, Mr Wedge, Billy Ball, Arthur Slater.

A drawing of Whiteladies Priory done in 1660, nine years after King Charles sought refuge there when fleeing from the Battle of Worcester. There was a farmhouse attached to one end, where he stayed but which has long since gone.

Blackladies Priory, a convent of black-robed Benedictine nuns, shown here in the last century. It became a farmhouse by then, and is still in use as such to this day.

Boscobel House, the home of the Pendrel family where King Charles moved after he left Whiteladies, only a kilometre away down the lane to Tong.

The door of Whiteladies Priory, which was founded around 1185, but fell into ruins soon after the Dissolution in 1538.

The ruins of Whiteladies remain today much as they did in the seventeenth century, and when this picture was taken before the First World War.

The dining room of Boscobel as it was between the wars, and as it is preserved now by the National Trust.

BOSCOBEL HOUSE
ENTRANCE TO SECRET PASSAGE AND CHIMNEY

The secret passage used by King Charles to hide from Parliamentary soldiers.

The famous King's Oak just outside Boscobel, in the branches of which King Charles is supposed to have hidden when the Roundheads were searching for him. Looking far too young a tree to be the actual one, it would, in the seventeenth century, have been one of many in the surrounding forest.

An aerial view of Weston Park, the Earl of Bradford's family home, photographed in 1935.

The rear of Weston Hall betweem the wars. Now open to the public, it also hosts many speacial events.

The village pump at Weston-under-Lizard, next to Weston Park, at around the turn of the century, The pump itself is now gone, but the structure is in use as a bus shelter,

During the Second World War a stretch of land at Weston Park was used by No. 9 M.U. at RAF Cosford as a Satellite Landing Ground for storing aircraft. This small Robin hangar was camouflaged to look like a country cottage. Most of the aircraft were stored under the trees of the estate.

This building, shown here in 1970, was used as the SLG office and to store the tractor which towed the aircraft from the grass strip. It stands next to the Tong-Bishop's Woods road, and has now been converted into a bungalow.

Arthur Parry with some of his cattle who farmed Whiteladies Farm, in the 1950s, next to the ruins of the Priory.

Arthur Parry with a combine harvester in one of his fields of wheat during the 1950s, and fittingly for the area, under an oak tree, not far from the one at Boscobel.

A fitting picture to end the book, combining the two dominant occupations of the area, agriculture and aviation. This is one of the earliest crop-spraying helicopters, a French Djinn, and with a French registration, on Whiteladies Farm. The pilot was Australian, and when the Parry's went on holiday to Australia one year, who should they bump into in a Melbourne street, but the self same pilot!

Acknowledgements

The search for photographs of the Albrighton and Shifnal area has been a great delight. I have met many people who were helpful, not least because many of them knew my father, John, my grandfather, Dan, or even my great-grandfather George. I was struck time and again by how many of the elder residents of the area knew one another, and could recognise one another in school photographs of seventy years ago. There was a close-knit community here, which sadly may soon be swamped by the large increases in population since the war.

The basis for the book was a large collection of picture postcards accumulated by my grandmother, Jane Brew, as well as family snapshots. In addition I have to thank all those who helped me and loaned me photographs. I hope I have included all their names below:

David Bate, Jim Boulton, The Boulton Paul Association, John and Leah Brew, Peter Brew, Revd David Chantrey, Dowty Aerospace Wolverhampton, Bess Edwards (librarian at Idsall School), Hurbert Ellis, Denis Hodgkiss, Maud Hawksworth, Ernie Howells, Doris Howells, Mary Humphreys, F. Jones, Gary Jones (headmaster, Albrighton County School), Joan Lees, Lockley's Garage, Alfred McAlpine Ltd, Mrs Gwen Matthias, Evelyn Paddon, Mrs Parry, Frances Plain, Bob Smith, Tommy Smith.